To Nancy and Bob Banker: May your skies be clear and
your days be filled with sunshine!

Peter Spier's
RAIN

Peter Spier's
RAIN

Doubleday & Company, Inc., Garden City, New York

Library of Congress Catalog Card Number 81-43056   ISBN 0-385-15484-4 Trade   0-385-15485-2 Prebound